HIDDEN DANGERS

SEEK AND FIND 13 OF THE WORLD'S *DEADLIEST* ANIMALS

written by **LOLA M. SCHAEFER**

illustrated by **TYMN ARMSTRONG**

chronicle books · san francisco

CAUTION

Like us, animals try to avoid danger. But if someone or something invades their territories or startles them, they'll use defense mechanisms to protect themselves. In some cases, that defense is nothing more than a harsh sting. Other times, it may be venomous tentacles, barbed quills, or poison-oozing skin.

Just like in the real world, you may not see all of the animals in this book at first glance. Take a few moments. Look under leaves, in the waves, or on a mountain ledge to find all of the creatures. **SOMETIMES DANGER IS RIGHT IN FRONT OF YOU.**

HOW MANY DEADLY ANIMALS ARE THERE?
Answers to the seek and find are on the last page.

Falling off a mountain with a deep, bleeding wound **WILL KILL YOU!** See that **MOUNTAIN GOAT** standing on the log? Look at those horns! They're sharp enough to rip skin and cut through flesh. Being rammed with those horns is brutal, or **DEADLY.** If you, or any other animal, intrude on a mountain goat's territory, it's going to defend itself with a good butt of its horns. If the goring doesn't cause a serious injury, and it usually does, falling down the face of a mountain will.

A mountain goat only protects itself if it feels **TRAPPED** or **THREATENED.** So always hike with friends or a guide, and stay on the marked trails. If a mountain goat should cross your path, remain calm. Hold still and study the trail behind you. Take a dozen slow steps backward, then turn and enjoy the return hike.

Want to be **DEAD IN JUST TWO MINUTES**? No? Then don't touch the bright, glistening skin on that frog. Most rainforest plants and animals will never hurt you, but the GOLDEN POISON DART FROG's skin is covered in a **TOXIN** that immediately attacks the nervous system of its enemies. If you touch this creature, the poison can numb your skin, your hand, and maybe your whole arm. If you accidentally get a drop or two of the toxin in your eyes, mouth, or an open sore, it will paralyze your lungs and stop your heart. You will be dead in minutes!

But this doesn't have to happen to you. When exploring, if you come close to a golden poison dart frog, **STOP**. Admire its tiny size and bright color, but remember that its skin is coated with enough poison to kill 8 to 20 people. Then, turn and walk away. The frog will not follow you, and you will have just seen the animal with **THE MOST DEADLY TOXIN IN THE WORLD.**

PRICKLY, PIERCING QUILLS jab skin! **OUCH!** The NORTH AMERICAN PORCUPINE is covered in 25,000 to 30,000 quills. If you approach one, it might rattle its quills as a warning. If you come closer, the porcupine will turn its back and push its quills to stand straight. Then it will **STRIKE** with its tail, ramming its quills into you. Your body heat will make the layers of tiny barbs on the tips of the quills expand, holding the quills in place. You may need pliers to pull them out!

When hiking through the woods or near a forest, keep an eye out for porcupines. They are mostly nocturnal, so if you hike at night, make sure you have a flashlight. Porcupines are slow-moving animals and will not attack unless you get too close or startle them. They only use their quills to defend themselves. If a porcupine crosses your path, **BACK AWAY!** Then, turn around and get out of there!

Don't crowd a shark. **A GREAT HAMMERHEAD**, like some other sharks, will defend its territory if threatened. **WITH ITS TEETH.** If one of these 500- to 1,000-pound (227- to 454-kilogram) creatures confuses you with an enemy or a tasty fish, swim . . . and swim fast! The hammerhead will strike with its head and bludgeon you again and again until you are weak and weary. Then it will open its powerful jaws and shred you with its serrated teeth. **YOU WILL BE DEAD.**

Some sharks, even hammerheads, occasionally come close to beaches. To avoid meeting one head-to-head, swim and boogie board with friends or family close to shore. If you are in the water and you see a dorsal fin or a shark head coming your way, remain calm. Yell "**HELP**" loudly two or three times. Walk or swim quickly to the beach or the nearest boat ladder. Your life depends on it!

WATCH OUT! A DEATHSTALKER SCORPION has its tail lifted over its head. That tail is **SHARP**, **PAINFUL**, and ready to **STING**, sending **VENOM** into its victim. Many scorpions live in warm, dry climates such as deserts or tropical grasslands. If you alarm or threaten one, it will raise its tail, jab its telson into you, and release venom into your body. This sting can cause many different reactions, including intense pain, swelling of the skin, numbness, and in some cases . . . **DEATH**.

Since scorpions are nocturnal and hide during the day, it's almost impossible to see them. Always examine a site well before setting up a tent or sitting on the ground. Rake away any loose bark, grass, or pebbles. If you do see a scorpion, **DON'T PANIC**. Just get away! If a scorpion crawls on your clothing or skin, shake it off. Don't swat it. If you ever get stung by a scorpion, treat it like a bee or wasp sting and immediately visit a doctor.

YEOW! The sting of the TARANTULA HAWK WASP will hurt—**HURT BADLY**—for two or three minutes. It is said to be the most painful sting of any wasp. And the skin around the puncture wound will **SWELL, THROB,** and **ITCH** with the venom for hours or days. The female tarantula hawk wasp is not an aggressive insect, but she will sting if threatened or provoked. One wasp sting is not life-threatening (unless you have an allergy to the venom). But unlike honeybees, one female wasp can sting again, and again, and again, and a whole swarm of wasps can sting you until you're dead!

Enjoy the outdoors, but be aware of wasps. If you see one coming near you, **BACK OFF** and wave your hands around your head to disturb the air around you (not to swat it). If you see a group of wasps, **STAY AWAY!** If you do get stung, treat the wound as you would any insect sting. Carefully remove the stinger, wash with soap and water, and apply ice to the area. However, if you are allergic to bee or wasp venom, take the proper medication immediately and tell an adult.

SLAP! An angry **ALLIGATOR** can whack you with a 200-pound (91-kilogram) tail, **GRAB** you with its large jaws, and drag you to the bottom of the river to **DROWN**. If you enter an American alligator's territory, this wetland creature defends itself with its tail first. If that doesn't knock you senseless, then it might decide to grab you with its jaws, which pack a force of 2,125 pounds (9,452 Newtons). **OUCH!** The alligator's final attack is to pull you underwater until you're dead.

When you're exploring swamps or marshes, remain on the wooden walkways and obey all signs. If you're traveling in a boat, keep your hands and feet inside. And, of course, never throw food to attract an alligator. If you meet an alligator on land, confuse it. Run right four or five steps, then left four or five steps, zigzagging back and forth. If possible, climb a tree or hide behind a large object. Alligators are **BIG** and **POWERFUL** (and surprisingly fast runners), but they are easily fooled.

DON'T FIGHT a 6,000-pound (2,722-kilogram), unpredictable **HIPPOPOTAMUS.** You **WON'T WIN!** Female and male hippos **ATTACK,** and sometimes without a reason or warning. If you are visiting Africa and get between a hippo and its source of water, get inside its territory, or get near a calf, you'll be sorry. Whether you're on land or in a boat, it will charge, bang its head into you again and again, then maul you with teeth that can be 1 foot (30 centimetres) long. That'll be it for you!

Did you know that **MORE PEOPLE ARE KILLED** every year by hippos than by sharks? To avoid this fate, stay far, far away from the home of the hippopotamus. The only safe way to view a hippo is from a jeep or a boat—a very fast one. Since a hippo can run nearly 20 miles (32 kilometres) per hour, you would need a quick getaway. **NEVER** get out of the vehicle for a closer look. It could be the last thing you ever do!

FANGS. Fangs that inject **VENOM.** Venom that kills! Snake bites always hurt, but the venomous bite of the **AQUATIC CORAL SNAKE** can kill within 30 minutes. This venom attacks the nervous system and paralyzes your lungs, which results in suffocation. The aquatic coral snake does not seek out fights, but it will defend itself. If you come too close, try to grab it, or step on it, the snake will strike.

When visiting the rainforest, make sure you are always with someone who is familiar with the plants and animals of the area. Wear thick, sturdy shoes, watch where you walk, and remain on marked trails. If you see a colorful snake with red and yellow stripes, **STOP.** Keep your hands to yourself and **STAY AWAY!** While in a boat, keep your hands and feet inside. If you leave the aquatic coral snake alone, it will be happy. So will you!

RIP! TEAR! SLASH! Better hope it's not your skin in the talons of a **BALD EAGLE**. If so, you're in trouble! Usually an eagle uses its talons to grab live prey. But if you come too close to its nest, its young, or the bird itself, it will lift one of its legs and extend four pointed talons. With one **SWIPE**, these **RAZOR-LIKE CLAWS** can tear open your chest or arm. The scratches are deep, painful, and the eagle's way of saying, leave me alone!

When climbing trees, be on the lookout for eagle nests. If you see one, climb back down. Since most eagles build their nests high up in trees or on poles, it's easier (and safer) to admire them from the ground. Eagles are majestic creatures **CAPABLE OF KILLING** a deer or a wolf. They are usually not interested in humans. Usually.

If a **MOOSE** charges, **BEWARE**. It could **STOMP** you with its hooves or **GORE** you with its antlers. A female moose will do anything to protect her calf. Weighing in at up to **900** pounds (**408** kilograms), she can knock you down with one hit of her body. She might then rise up on her back hooves and bring her front hooves crashing down on you. A male is aggressive during mating season and will charge with his antlers to maul, stab, or throw you around like a rag doll. You might live, but you might not!

Since the number of moose is increasing, it's a lot more likely that you might see one while hiking in or near Alaska or Canada. If a moose starts to come your way, turn and **RUN** away! Usually it will stop running after a short distance. But if the moose doesn't slow up, **HIDE!** Hide behind a large tree trunk or rock. Roll into a tight ball, placing your arms over your head for protection. When the moose cannot see you, it will walk away. Later, so can you!

Six thousand inches (15,240 centimetres) of **TENTACLES** that **STING, PUNCTURE,** and **KILL!** This is the nightmare in store for the person who comes in contact with the **AUSTRALIAN BOX JELLYFISH.** This creature will defend itself by draping some of its 60 tentacles against your skin. Each tentacle is covered in thousands of stinging capsules that fire tiny tubes, or harpoons, into your skin and deposit deadly venom. This toxin attacks the heart, skin, and nerves, which causes you to go into shock and **DIE WITHIN MINUTES.**

If you visit northern Australia, stay out of the ocean. The box jellyfish lives in the coastal waters all around that side of the country. Their numbers are higher from October to May, but they are always present. Since it is almost **IMPOSSIBLE** to see the tentacles in the water before they touch your skin, stay on shore. If you are ever close to a box jellyfish, let's hope it is on the other side of a glass wall in an aquarium.

SCRATCH! SCRAPE! SLASH! If you get too close to a **GRIZZLY BEAR**, your arms and legs could be **RIPPED** beyond repair with just one swipe of its claws. When a grizzly is cornered, surprised, or protecting cubs, it might first roar or run toward you, then turn away. If it still feels threatened, the bear will then **CHARGE**. The claws on its front paws are 3 to 4 inches (7.5 to 10 centimetres) long. These are the claws that the grizzly bear will use to maul, scrape, and tear.

Stay away from grizzly bears! If you are hiking where there are grizzlies, carry bear spray and try to make some noise as you hike. Grizzlies will often avoid people if they hear them coming. You do **NOT** want to surprise a grizzly bear. If you meet one in the wild, stand still. If the bear does not approach you, back away slowly. If it does approach, use your bear spray on its head. Then **RUN AWAY**.

BE PREPARED

Whenever you are out exploring, hiking, or canoeing, be prepared. For what? For any kind of accident or mishap. If you are out of sight of a nature center, lodge, or mini-mart, it's wise to have a few safety items with you. Just in case. Pack your backpack with these essentials to guarantee a safe and speedy return.

WATER Carry 18 to 24 ounces (530 to 710 millilitres) of water per person for every 3 to 4 hours you plan on being out in nature. This will provide enough water for drinking, as well as additional water in case you need to clean a wound.

BANDAGES Always carry eight to ten bandages for blisters or wounds.

ENERGY BARS or NUTS-AND-DRIED-FRUIT TRAIL MIX You'll use a lot of calories while out hiking, especially if you have to do any running away or have to spend longer outdoors than you planned. It's good to have a quick and easy snack that will give you a boost of energy.

CELL PHONE Someone in your group needs to have a phone so you can call for help if needed.

SIGNAL FLAG or FLARE In case of an extreme emergency where you cannot move from your location, you can wave a signal flag or launch a flare into the evening sky to help a rescue team find you.

FLASHLIGHT You might find yourself hiking after dark or through a cave. A flashlight will help you stay on a safe path.

ROPE or **CORD** Bring a 5- to 7-foot (1.5- to 2-metre) length of rope in case you need to hoist, support, tie, bundle, carry, or climb.

MAP, COMPASS, or **GPS** It's easy to get turned around, especially when you're not familiar with the area. Make a mental note of landmarks as you travel so you can look for those landmarks on your return trip. If that fails, any of these three items will help you get back on course.

ANTIBIOTIC CREAM or **SPRAY** Use this on a wound before applying a bandage.

ANTI-ITCH CREAM Depending on the time of year, you could run into a wide variety of insects and creepy crawlers. If you should get a painful sting or bite, these creams will help reduce swelling and itching.

MATCHES If you are lost or need to remain out during the night, a campfire can provide warmth, security, a way to cook food, and a light to help others find you.

ANTISEPTIC WIPES These will come in handy if anyone falls and has an abrasion, or if you need to clean a drinking or eating surface.

LOUD WHISTLE One person needs to carry a whistle in case the cell phone doesn't work and you need to alert someone to your location. It can also be used as a warning signal.

POISON. VENOM. WHAT'S THE DIFFERENCE?

As it turns out, poison and venom are quite similar in their chemical makeup, and in some cases they're identical substances. Both poisons and venoms are toxins. The difference between the two is in how they are delivered to other creatures.

Poisonous animals, such as the golden poison dart frog and puffer fish, use their toxins mostly to discourage or ward off predators. The poison is transferred to another creature by absorption through touching, inhalation by sniffing, or ingestion when licked or eaten.

Venomous animals, such as the deathstalker scorpion and the aquatic coral snake, use their toxins mostly to capture and kill prey. Venom is different from poison because it is injected from the host animal into another creature. Fangs, telsons, spines, barbs, spurs, harpoons, or the animal's teeth deliver the venom directly into the skin or bloodstream of their prey.

The Asian tiger snake is very unusual because unlike most animals, it is poisonous and venomous. This snake produces both a venom, which it injects with its fangs, and a poison, which it secretes around its neck and can be absorbed by the touch of an enemy. Avoid this animal. It's double trouble.

Pop Quiz: What do you think? Are toxic plants poisonous or venomous? Answer on facing page.

For my father, R. L. Bennett,
who taught me to respect
animals in the wild
—L. M. S.

For Nova
—T. A.

Text copyright © 2017 by Lola M. Schaefer.
Illustrations copyright © 2017 by Tymn Armstrong.
All rights reserved. No part of this book may be
reproduced in any form without written permission from
the publisher.

Library of Congress Cataloging-in-Publication Data:
Schaefer, Lola M., 1950- | Armstrong, Tymn, illustrator.
Hidden dangers : seek and find 13 of the world's deadliest
animals / by Lola M. Schaefer ; illustrated by Tymn
Armstrong.
Description: San Francisco, California : Chronicle Books,
LLC, [2017] |
Audience: Age 5-8. | Audience: K to grade 3.
Identifiers: LCCN 2016002186 | ISBN 9781452134291
(alk. paper)
Subjects: LCSH: Dangerous animals—Juvenile
literature.

Classification: LCC QL100 .S33 2017 | DDC 591.6/5—dc23
LC record available at http://lccn.loc.gov/2016002186

Manufactured in China.

MIX
Paper from
responsible sources
FSC™ C104723

Design by Amelia Mack and Tymn Armstrong.
Typeset in Metallophile.
The illustrations in this book were rendered digitally.

10 9 8 7 6 5 4 3 2 1

Chronicle Books LLC
680 Second Street
San Francisco, California 94107
www.chroniclekids.com

ANSWERS: MOUNTAIN GOATS: 23. GOLDEN POISON DART FROGS: 13. NORTH AMERICAN PORCUPINES: 10. GREAT HAMMERHEAD SHARKS: 5. DEATHSTALKER SCORPIONS: 24. TARANTULA HAWK WASPS: 7. HIPPOPOTAMI: 12. AQUATIC CORAL SNAKES: 10. BALD EAGLES: 12. MOOSE: 10. AUSTRALIAN BOX JELLYFISH: 26. GRIZZLY BEARS: 1 ANGRY MOTHER BEAR (that's enough) AND 2 CUBS. POISONOUS OR VENOMOUS? POISONOUS.